I Hate Goodbyes!

By

Kathleen C. Szaj

Illustrated by

Mark A. Hicks

Paulist Press
New York / Mahwah, N.J.

Illustrations copyright © 1996 by Mark A. Hicks

For my parents, my family, and my friends.
M.A.H.

Library of Congress Cataloging-in-Publication Data

Szaj, Kathleen C.
    I hate goodbyes! / by Kathleen C. Szaj; illustrated by Mark A. Hicks.
      p. cm.
    ISBN 0-8091-6635-6 (alk. paper)
    1. Grief in children.   2. Separation (Psychology) in children.
  3. Loss (Psychology) in children.   4. Children—Counseling of.
  I. Title.
  BF723.G75S83   1996
  155.4'124—dc20   96-22276
                                           CIP

Published by Paulist Press
997 Macarthur Boulevard
Mahwah, New Jersey 07430

Printed and bound in the
United States of America

To Marvin Kaye,
catalyst, critic,
colleague and friend
and
to Isabella Reese
and Katie Marburger,
to whom I hate
saying goodbye.

I hate goodbyes . . .

. . . even more
than going to bed
when it's still light outside.

I hate goodbyes so much, I decided
to make all goodbyes disappear.

One day, my daddy said, "Goodbye, Katie. I'm off to catch my train to work in the city. Why don't you think of a story that I can read to you when I come back tomorrow night, okay?"

Do you know what I did? I did NOT think of a story for my daddy to read to me. I sang "A Spoonful of Sugar" (which I had just learned) in my LOUDEST voice. Singing in a loud voice should make goodbyes disappear. Right?

I hate goodbye words . . .

. . . more than biting into cookies
that LOOK like chocolate chip cookies
but are really full of raisins.

. . . even more than being told
a hundred times, "DON'T SCRATCH
THOSE CHICKEN POX, KATIE!"
when I just couldn't stand that
horrible itching, especially
behind my ears and
between my toes.

I hate goodbye words so much,
I decided to make all
goodbye people disappear.

One day, my granny and grandpa said, "Goodbye, Katie. We're off to the airport to catch our plane that will take us home. We'll miss you, dear, but we're SO glad we'll be seeing you at Thanksgiving. Now give us a hug and kiss, won't you?"

Do you know what I did? I did NOT give hugs and kisses to Granny and Grandpa. I grabbed Pippie, my naughtiest teddy bear, and scolded him GOOD and LOUD for saying he wanted spaghetti bolognese for dinner AGAIN. Scolding stubborn teddies should make people with goodbye words disappear. Right?

I really hate goodbye feelings . . .

... more than tripping on the gym mat when I tried doing a perfect cartwheel for my first Parents' Day performance.

. . . more than finding out that Peter,
who used to be my best friend
last summer, now likes to play
with toy trucks much better
than he likes playing
with me.

. . . even more
than hearing, "No more
talking, Katie. It's VERY late—PLEASE
go to sleep now," when I really want my mummy
to stay and talk with me some more.

I hate goodbye feelings so much,

I decided to make ALL feelings disappear.

One day,
my mummy said,
"Goodbye, Katie.
My taxi will be
here soon to
take me to my
conference.
But don't worry,
honey, I'll be
back before you
know it. What
kind of present
should I bring
back for you?"

Do you know
what I did? I did
NOT think of the
present I wanted
Mummy to bring

me. I checked to see how many loose teeth I had so far and
wiggled the loosest ones EXTRA HARD. Wiggling loose teeth
extra hard so they almost fall out should make goodbye words
and goodbye people and goodbye feelings disappear. Right?

I really, really
hate goodbyes.

I tried to make my daddy's words disappear,
but somehow they sneaked inside
my ears and made me
hear anyway.

I tried to make my granny
and grandpa disappear,
but I STILL saw
them wave
goodbye
to me.

I tried to make ALL my
feelings disappear, but I
felt my heart get hurt when
it fell PLOP! down into my
stomach after I heard my
mummy's taxi door
slam shut.

One day, all the
goodbye words and the
goodbye people and the
goodbye feelings hiding
deep inside my body
moved right up and
waited behind
my eyes.

This time when my mummy said goodbye,
I cried and cried . . . enough to fill Granny's
deep swimming pool, I think.

Daddy hugged me and asked me
if I felt better. I said,
"Maybe a teensy bit. But, I STILL
hate goodbyes."

Do you know what my daddy said?
He told me that I'm not the only one
who hates goodbyes. My granny,
grandpa, mummy and
daddy ALL hate
goodbyes. More
than anything
else in the
whole world.
Just like me.

We all wish
we could make
goodbyes disappear
forever. But not even
grown-ups who love
me a lot know how.
They only know how
to come back as
soon as they can . . .
and to say our silly
goodbye words.

Whenever they have to
tell me goodbye, my mummy,
daddy, granny or grandpa
say, "See you later, my
KATER-GATOR."

Do you know what I do?
I answer, "In a little while,
with your crocodile
smile."

Sometimes I still cry
when they tell me those
goodbyes. But REAL tears
should help pretend alligators
and make-believe crocodiles feel a
teensy bit better.

Right?